This Book

is dedicated to

my sons

Nathan

and

Jake

DRC PUBLISHING

3 Parliament Street
St. John's, Newfoundland and Labrador
A1A 2Y6
Telephone: (709) 726-0960
E-mail: staceypj@nl.rogers.com
www.drcpublishingnl.com

© Dale Ryan

Library and Archives Canada Cataloguing in Publication

Ryan, Dale
The Newfoundland and Labrador ABC
alphabet book / Dale Ryan.

ISBN 978-1-926689-28-9

1. English language--Alphabet--Juvenile literature.
2. Newfoundland and Labrador--Pictorial works--Juvenile
literature. 3. Alphabet books. I. Title.

PE1155.R93 2010   j421'.1   C2010-906378-3

All original paintings by Dale Ryan

Published 2010
Printed in Canada

Newfoundland and Labrador

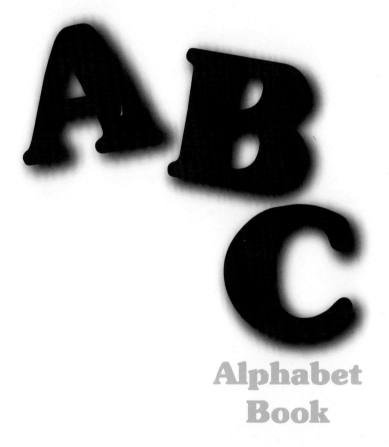

Alphabet
Book

A is for the Atlantic
off the coast of
Newfoundland

B is for bread
she makes with
her hands

C is for cod
drying on shore

D is for dory
with two wooden oars

E is for early
when he gets out of bed

F is for fence
around the old homestead

G is for grandfather loading a cart with hay

H is for hand bar
used back in the day

I is for iceberg let's all take a look

©DaleRyan '10

K is for killick

made of sticks and a ston

L is for lighthouse
that stands all alone

M is for mending
the holes in the net

N is for Newfoundland dog
a friend and a pet

O is for oven
on an old wood stove

P is for puffins
that play in the cove

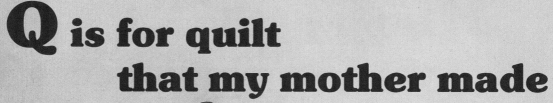

Q is for quilt
that my mother made

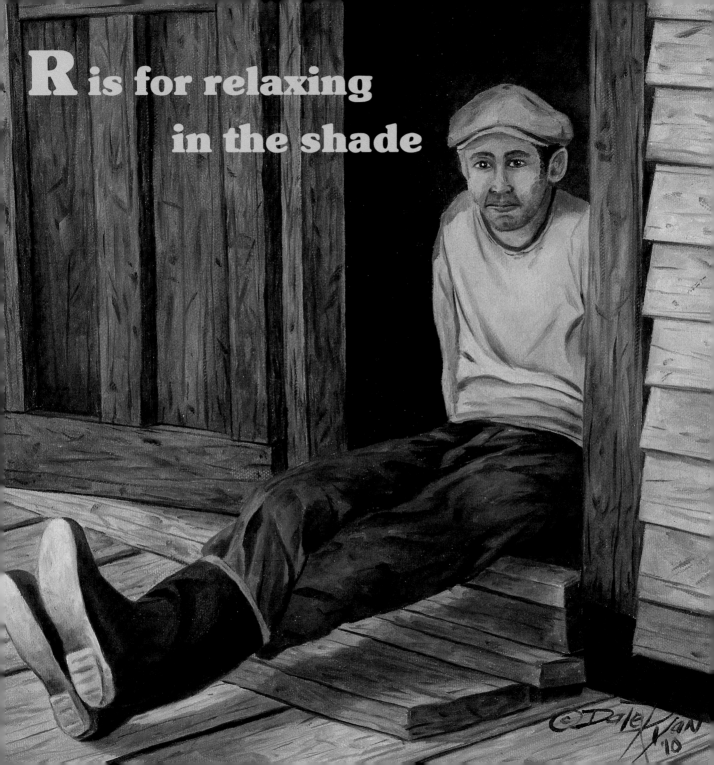

R is for relaxing
in the shade

S is for saltbox
a house and a home

T is for twine needle made of an old whale bone

U is for underwater
where the whales do play

V is for very
a very nice day

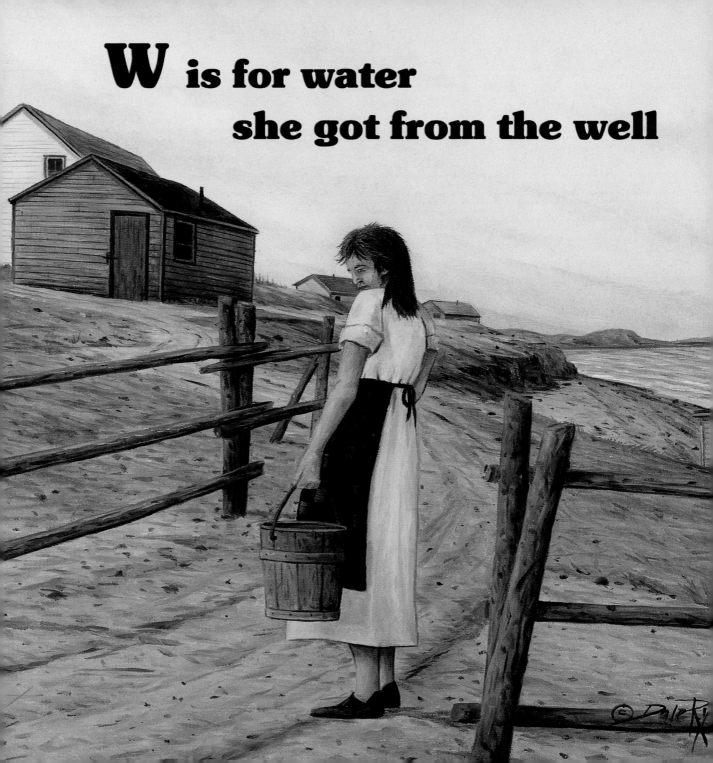

W is for water
she got from the well

X is in exit
they all had their fill

Y is for yarn
to knit hats for our heads

Z is in snooze on his water bed

The End

All illustrations in this book can be purchased as Art Prints. For more information call Dale at 709-782-4669 or 709-743-3662

To view and purchase any of these originals and canvas edition prints please visit Step-A-Side Art Gallery in Heritage Square, Burin, NL. For more information please call 709-891-2345.

NATHAN AND FRIENDS

Written and Illustrated by Dale Ryan

To purchase this book call Dale at 709-782-4669 or 709-743-3662
or DRC Publishing at 709-726-0960
$9.95